AIRCRAFT CARRIERS

KEVIN DOYLE

Lerner Publications Company
Minneapolis

Lerner Publications Company.
A division of Lerner Publishing Group
241 First Avenue North
Minneapolis, MN55401 U.S.A.

Website address: www.lernerbooks.com

Library of Congress Cataloging-in-Publication Data

Doyle, Kevin.
  Aircraft carriers / by Kevin Doyle.
      p. cm. -- (Military hardware in action)
Includes index.
Summary: Profiles some of the different aircraft carriers used by the
United States Navy and other navies around the world, describing their
designs, aircraft, weapons, and uses.
  ISBN 0–8225–4702–3 ((lib. bdg.)
1. Aircraft carriers--United States--Juvenile literature. 2. Aircraft
carriers--Juvenile literature. [1. Aircraft carriers.] I. Title.
II. Series.
  V874.3 .D69 2003
  359.9'4835--dc21   2002013597

Printed in China
Bound in the United States of America
1 2 3 4 5 6 – OS—08 07 06 05 04 03

This book uses black and yellow chevrons as a decorative element on some headers. They do not point to other elements on the page.

Contents

Introduction

The F/A18 Hornet rushes violently forward with a roar in a swirl of hissing steam. In less than three seconds, the plane's 50,000 pounds of metal and electronics hurtle from 0 to 130 miles per hour into a blue sky. Flying combat aircraft from the flight deck (an aircraft carrier's take off and landing space) is the most exhilarating, demanding, and challenging job in military aviation.

BLAST OFF

More like a rocket than an airplane, this F/A18 Hornet reaches flying speed in under three seconds. Takeoff is aided by a powerful steam **catapult** fitted along the flight deck.

>> **catapult** = a device that rapidly propels the airplane along the deck

Shaky Start

Even before World War I (1914–1918), naval commanders were quick to see the benefits of launching aircraft off the deck of a ship. High in the sky, an aerial observer can see enemy vessels long before they appear over the horizon. Sea trials began as early as 1910, using converted warships and fragile **biplanes**.

FILE OF FIRSTS

First deck launch:
Eugene Ely in Curtiss biplane from USS *Birmingham*, 1910

First deck landing:
Ely in Curtiss biplane on USS *Pennsylvania*, 1911

First purpose-built carrier:
HMS *Argus*, 1917

LANDING ON

Aviation pioneer Eugene Ely made the first successful deck landing in 1911. His Curtiss biplane landed on a platform built over the deck of the USS *Pennsylvania*.

PURPOSE-BUILT

The U.S. Navy's first specially built carrier was the USS *Langley*. It was launched in 1922. It consisted of a full-length flight deck built over the hull of an old fleet supply ship.

>> **biplane** = an airplane with double-decker wings

World Wars

Naval aviation remained mostly experimental through World War I. Only **floatplanes** were used in active service. They were lowered into or raised from the water by cranes fixed to the ship's deck. Along with airships and towed balloons, floatplanes were used for observation. By World War II (1939–1945), aircraft carriers had become a major part of the world's leading navies.

PEARL HARBOR

On December 7, 1941, the Japanese raided the U.S. Pacific Fleet stationed at Pearl Harbor on the Hawaiian island of Oahu. The raid was only possible because Japanese aircraft carriers steamed across the Pacific to get within reach. The attack brought the United States into World War II.

>> **floatplane** = an airplane that can take off and land on water

Postwar Race

World War II had shown the importance of aircraft carriers in long-range operations. The post-World War II era saw the United States and its Western European allies pitted against the Soviet Union and its Eastern European allies. The Soviet Navy began a rapid program of building aircraft carriers. It was trying to catch up with the United States and other Western nations.

SOVIET EXPANSION

The Soviet aircraft carrier *Kiev*, photographed by a **reconnaissance** aircraft during the 1980s

Korea and Vietnam

Aircraft carriers gave the United States and its allies control of distant seas during both the Korean War (1950–1953) and the war in Vietnam (1965–1975). These operations would not have been possible without control over sea routes and the airspace above the oceans.

INDOCHINA

An F4 Phantom leaps from the deck of the USS *Saratoga* during the Vietnam War. Over 3,000 missions were flown from the "Sara" stationed in the Gulf of Tonkin.

REACHING OUT

Modern **carrier groups** include several dozen ships and more than 200 aircraft. They bring the might of a nation's military strength to almost anywhere in the world. The U.S. Navy has had a leading role in international operations since the end of World War II.

City at Sea

A carrier group at sea resembles a small floating city. It requires constant supplies of fuel, food, and personnel to remain effective. Supply and combat support ships keep the carrier group ready. This ensures that a fleet can respond quickly to changing conflicts and political events.

The Carrier's Job

The **strategic** role of the aircraft carrier is to provide a floating airbase that can deliver air power to almost anywhere in the world. Because of carriers, strike aircraft and cruise missiles can be launched without the need for ground forces or a land assault. Carriers also provide aircraft in places where ground or surface forces need air support.

18-YEAR AIRBASE

The USS *Dwight D. Eisenhower* is a military airbase at sea. This state-of-the-art nuclear-powered carrier has unlimited range, since it only needs refueling every 18 years.

CLEARING THE AIR

Providing freedom to use airspace is the most important **tactical** job of the carrier fleet. Fleet aircraft and missiles create an invisible umbrella hundreds of miles across that protect forces from attack. This U.S. Navy F14 Tomcat fighter has a patrol range of 2,000 miles.

>> **strategic** – relating to political or long-term military goals

Policing the World

Aircraft carriers and their fleet support ships act as an international police force. They can respond to UN peacekeeping needs, for example. Since 2000 tensions in eastern Europe, the Middle East, and the Indian subcontinent have all involved U.S. carrier fleets in peacekeeping missions.

TASK FORCE

Ships of the U.S. Navy's Task Force 155 include the aircraft carriers USS *America* and USS *John F. Kennedy*. The group was stationed in the Red Sea during Operation Desert Storm in 1991.

THIRSTY

The carrier USS *John F. Kennedy (left)* receives fuel from the fast combat support ship USS *Seattle*. Being able to refuel at sea enables ships of a U.S. Navy carrier group to be wherever they are needed, for as long as they are needed.

Aircraft Types

There are three main types of carrier aircraft: conventional, vertical takeoff and landing (VTOL), and vertical or short takeoff and landing (VSTOL). Conventional airplanes have fixed wings like the F/A18 or **variable geometry** like the F14. They need a long flight deck to take off and land. VTOL aircraft, mainly helicopters, need only a small deck. VSTOL refers to **vectored-thrust** airplanes such as the AV8 Harrier and the new Joint Strike Fighter (JSF).

AV8 HARRIER

A U.S. Marine Corps AV8 Harrier VSTOL strike fighter. It has the capacity to take off and land vertically. This is very costly in fuel. It also reduces the range and weapon load the plane can carry. Short takeoffs on a short-deck carrier can reduce this problem.

>> **variable geometry** = wings that sweep back in high-speed flight

Carrier Types

To launch conventional airplanes, carriers need full-length flight decks. The planes require catapults to take off and arrester wires to stop when landing. Smaller carriers and other types of ship can operate VTOL aircaft. To fly VSTOL aircraft, ships still need a flight deck, but it is relatively short and often has a "ski-lift" or ramp at the front to help planes take off.

VSTOL CARRIERS

This British "through-deck" carrier is designed to operate VSTOL aircraft. It has a short, straight deck with a ramp at the front.

ANGLE-DECK CARRIERS

The USS *Kitty Hawk* is a conventional angle-deck carrier. This design allows two runways to operate at the same time. The angle deck is fitted with a catapult and is used for taking off. The straight or through deck is fitted with arrester wires and is used for landings.

Carrier Crews

A full-sized aircraft carrier such as the USS *Nimitz* has a crew of about 6,000. The men and women on board have many jobs. Some are air crews, aircraft engineers, and aircraft maintenance staff. Other crews monitor flight-deck safety. Still others oversee and supply weapons to aircraft.

BELOW DECKS

Working in the orange glare of sodium lights, engineers keep aircraft like this F/A18 Hornet ready for combat in hangars below the flight deck. The airplanes are brought to the deck by large open elevators.

>> **amphibious assault ship** – a ship with landing craft to put troops ashore

Navy Crew

A carrier is also a warship and requires a full crew of regular sailors, engineers, and technicians. It also needs support personnel such as cooks, medical staff, and storekeepers. At the top, the captain and commanders take overall responsibility.

ALL HANDS ON DECK

The crew of the **amphibious assault ship** USS *Wasp* assemble on the flight deck.

COLOR CODES

Flight-deck crews all wear color-coded jackets that identify the kind of jobs they do. Red is for weapons handlers. Yellow stands for aircraft movement directors. The safety crew wears white. Deck equipment personnel have green jackets. Purple is for fuelers, and brown is for maintenance staff.

HARDWARE HANDLERS

A weapons crew in red shirts loads **HARM** missiles onto Corsair IIs aboard the USS *John F. Kennedy*.

>> **HARM** = heat-seeking anti-radiation missile

Air Crew

The men and women who pilot and crew the aircraft on a carrier are an elite group with unique skills. They fly powerful jet airplanes and helicopters from a small and often crowded space. Their tasks include strike and aerial combat, and anti-submarine warfare (ASW). They are called upon to perform high-tech reconnaissance, search and rescue, and air transport.

PILOT'S EYE VIEW

The gently moving deck looks tiny to a pilot. The flier lines up to land a twin-engined F14 Tomcat weighing 55,000 pounds and approaching at a speed of 125 mph. The landing deck is just 300 yards long, compared to a conventional airport runway of two miles or longer.

>> **hover** = to fly in the air above a fixed point without moving

HELICOPTER HAZARDS

A Sea King lands on an amphibious assault ship carrier. The flight crew must control the **hover** so as to keep the whirling rotors clear of the ship's **superstructure**.

LOOKING AHEAD

The crew aboard these carrier-based Grumman E6 Prowlers maintain a constant watch over the skies above and ahead of the fleet.

NIGHT FLYING

Landing an F14 Tomcat on an aircraft carrier deck at night is the most demanding challenge of all.

Carrier Weapons

The main weapons on an aircraft carrier are the aircraft themselves. They include strike, fighter, anti-submarine, and surveillance airplanes and helicopters. These in turn carry missiles, bombs, torpedoes, mines, and **depth charges.** Carriers may also carry attack weapons—such as cruise missiles—and defensive hardware, including anti-aircraft missiles, anti-missile missiles, and close-range guns.

STRIKE AIRCRAFT

The U.S. Navy's main strike aircraft is the F/A18 Hornet. It carries a range of weapons, including Sidewinder anti-aircraft missiles at the tip of its wings. The Navy F/A18 also carries up to 13,000 pounds of bombs and ground-attack missiles.

CORSAIR

A weapons crew prepares to load air interception missiles and bombs. The weapons are supplied to an A7 Corsair II attack aircraft based on the carrier USS *John F. Kennedy.* The aircraft carrier took part in an exercise in the Persian Gulf in 1991.

>> **depth charge** = an undersea bomb used against submarines

COMBAT AIRCRAFT

Flight crews on the deck of USS *Independence* cheer as one of their aircraft breaks the sound barrier during a low-level pass. The Mach 2.3 F14 Tomcat (*right*) is the world's leading carrier-borne **air-to-air combat** fighter. The F14 can carry Sparrow, Sidewinder, and Phoenix missiles.

VTOL AIRCRAFT

A Marine Corps AV8 Harrier lands vertically on the short flight deck of a U.S. Navy amphibious assault ship. The Harrier is a multirole airplane. It flies both strike and air combat missions with weapon loads of 9,000 pounds.

>> **air-to-air combat** = combat between aircraft in flight

Invisible beneath the surface of the ocean, an enemy submarine may be out of sight. But it must never be out of mind. Modern warships—and aircraft carriers in particular—are the first line of defense against this hidden threat.

VIKING

A **plane director** guides an air anti-submarine squadron S3 Viking onto the flight-deck catapult of the carrier USS *Independence*.

Helicopters

The helicopter takes a leading role in anti-submarine warfare and can match the speed of an underwater enemy. It can hover over the ocean and drop **sensor equipment** to detect engine or propeller noise.

HOVER POWER

Marine UH1 helicopters and AV8 Harriers wait on the deck of the amphibious assault ship USS *Nassau*. These vessels combine anti-submarine warfare tasks with an ability to launch ground troops ashore in landing craft.

SEA KING

A Sea King ASW helicopter lands on the deck of USS *Saratoga.* Beside the landing space sits an E2 Hawkeye early warning (EW) airplane with folded wings. These two aircraft offer a powerful defense against underwater or airborne attacks.

METAL DETECTOR

This U.S. Navy Sea King is lowering a magnetic detection buoy into the ocean. This equipment can sense magnetic changes caused by large metal objects, like submarines, below the surface.

Deck Weapons

As well as aircraft, the carrier has additional weapons mounted on its deck for attack and defense. Tomahawk cruise missiles and Harpoon ship-launched anti-aircraft missiles (SLAMs) can strike ground targets up to 600 miles away. Carriers also have weapons to defend themselves against submarine attacks, surface or air-launched missiles, and bombers.

TOMAHAWK

A ship-launched cruise missile. These long-range **guided missiles**, which can carry nuclear warheads, fly close to the ground. They are almost impossible to detect by **radar**.

Hitting Back

Aircraft carriers are at the center of a carrier task group. Many combat support ships and aircraft help to protect the carriers. Even if an enemy aircraft or submarine is able to slip past the outer defenses, the carrier is still equipped for close-in self-defense.

SEE AND TELL

An E2 Hawkeye EW airplane returns from a patrol. The task of a carrier-based surveillance aircraft such as the Hawkeye is not to engage the enemy directly. Rather, the plane is loaded with sophisticated electronics that enable it to find approaching danger.

SEA SPARROW

A RIM7 Sea Sparrow missile blasts out of its launcher aboard the USS *John F. Kennedy*. It can attack high-performance strike aircraft and missiles.

LAST RESORT

A Phalanx automatic radar-directed deck gun fires at an approaching intruder. If the outer defenses fail to stop an attacker, the rapid-fire automatic gun system can direct an accurate stream of explosive 20mm shells.

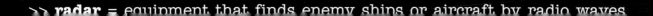

radar = equipment that finds enemy ships or aircraft by radio waves

23

Carriers in Action

Aircraft carriers have come a long way since the first biplanes struggled off converted **cruisers** before World War I. By World War II, battles fought around carrier groups shaped the course of the Pacific war. By the end of the 1900s, carriers had become the launching platforms for long-range, large-scale military actions all over the world.

WORLD WAR I

A British Royal Navy floatplane during the Battle of Jutland in June 1916. Carrier aviation was still new when the only major sea battle of World War I took place between British and German warships. After Jutland, the German Imperial Fleet lacked the confidence to take on the British navy.

>> **cruiser** = a large warship that carries a range of weapons

World War II

The United States, Great Britain, and Japan each operated aircraft carriers during World War II. All carried propeller-driven airplanes with **fixed wings.**

JAPAN ATTACKS

The USS *Shaw* explodes during the raid on Pearl Harbor. Japan attacked the Pacific Fleet as it lay at anchor. The Imperial Japanese Navy was well equipped at the time and already had combat experience against China.

ATTACKER'S EYE VIEW

A photograph taken from a Japanese carrier-based bomber during the raid on Pearl Harbor. Smoke rises from Hickam Field in the background.

"TORA, TORA..."

"One by one I counted them. Yes, the battleships were there all right, eight of them! But our last hope of finding any carriers was now gone. Not one was to be seen. It was 0749 when I ordered my radioman to send the command, 'Attack!' He began tapping out the code signal: 'Tora, Tora, Tora...'"

Commander Mitsuo Fuchida, Japanese navy pilot, Pearl Harbor attack leader

Midway

The Battle of Midway fought near Midway Island in the Pacific in June 1942 was the most decisive sea battle in U.S. history. After Pearl Harbor, Japanese navy commander Admiral Yamamoto planned to trap and destroy the rest of the U.S. Pacific Fleet. **Codebreakers** managed to read Japanese radio messages, and the fleet commander, Admiral Chester Nimitz, was ready for the attack. The Japanese gambled with almost their entire fleet. When they were defeated, they could no longer challenge the United States at sea.

DECK DAMAGE

A fire crew inspects bomb damage on the smoldering deck of the USS *Yorktown* during the Battle of Midway. The *Yorktown* later sank while being towed back to Pearl Harbor.

HIRYU

The Japanese carrier *Hiryu*, with a Nakajima B5N "Kate" torpedo bomber taking off. The *Hiryu* was sunk by aircraft from the USS *Yorktown* and the USS *Enterprise*.

>> **codebreaker** = a person who deciphers secret radio messages

"At 1222 I started the attack, rolling in a half-roll and coming to a steep 70-degree dive. About halfway down, anti-aircraft fire began booming around us—our approach being a complete surprise up to that point. As we neared our bomb-dropping point, another stroke of luck met our eyes. Both enemy carriers had their decks full of planes which had just returned from the attack on Midway."

Lieutenant Commander C. Wade McClusky U.S. Navy, Douglas **SBD** Dauntless pilot

South Atlantic

In 1982 Argentine forces invaded and occupied Britain's tiny Falkland Islands dependency in the South Atlantic. A British Carrier Task Force of 100 ships sailed 8,000 miles around the world to recover the islands. Argentina's only aircraft carrier, the *Veinticinco de Mayo*, was kept in port by fear of British submarine attack.

INVINCIBLE >>

The British through-deck carrier HMS *Invincible*. Harrier VTOL aircraft from the carriers *Invincible* and *Hermes* stopped Argentine navy pilots from sinking Task Force ships. British land forces retook the islands after 10 weeks.

Middle East Action

The Middle East has been a flashpoint since the end of World War II. Aircraft carriers from the United States and other countries have been involved in many recent operations to restore peace or to combat terrorism.

GULF WAR

The USS *Saratoga* heads for the Persian Gulf following the invasion of Kuwait by neighboring Iraq in 1990. An international **coalition**, led by the United States, was formed to get the invaders out. There were three U.S. aircraft carriers in the area at the time. They supplied 20 percent of the allied air combat strength during Operation Desert Storm.

INTRUDER

During operations to free Kuwait in 1991, a Grumman E6 Prowler hurtles down the deck of the USS *Saratoga*, with an F/A18 Hornet ready to follow.

Enduring Freedom

Following the September 11, 2001, attacks on the United States, Operation Enduring Freedom was launched. Its goal was to destroy the al-Qaeda terrorist organization in Afghanistan.

AGAINST TERROR

A deck crewman steps back as an F/A18 Hornet roars off the flight deck of the USS *Carl Vinson* to attack terrorist camps in Afghanistan.

>> **al-Qaeda** = an extremist terrorist organization led by Osama bin Laden

Airbase at Sea

Modern aircraft carriers have all the elements that make up an airbase. Carriers also need all the equipment and personnel required to keep a major warship at sea. Nimitz is the U.S. Navy's most advanced carrier class.

USS *Nimitz*

The USS *Nimitz* was named after Fleet Admiral Chester W. Nimitz, commander of the Pacific Fleet during World War II and hero of Midway. The ship began service in 1975 and was the first of its class. It has had several **refits** since launch. The nuclear-powered carrier has been active in the Atlantic, the Pacific, the Middle East, and the Mediterranean. In 2002 there were nine carriers in the Nimitz class.

FLOATING CITY

The USS *Nimitz* has a crew of more than 3,000 men and women, plus an additional 3,000 when the **air wing** is on board. *Nimitz* reaches over 18 stories high from keel to mast (bottom to top). The flight deck area covers 4.5 acres.

>> **refit** = a major overhaul or upgrade

CONTROL ROOM

A navy air traffic control officer monitors aircraft positions during missions from the USS *Nimitz*.

THEY ALSO SERVE

A medical officer gives a sailor a jab against possible germ warfare. Besides a fully equipped medical section, the *Nimitz* also has a movie theater, a barber shop, a laundry, a chapel, shops, gym equipment, and all the facilities normally found on a land base.

>> **air wing** = personnel who command, fly, and maintain the aircraft

USS *John C. Stennis*

The USS *John C. Stennis* is one of the navy's newest carriers. It is named after the Mississippi senator who was a keen supporter of naval strength. The carrier weighs 100,000 tons and is powered by two nuclear reactor engines. The engines run for 22 years before needing to refuel. They generate energy sufficient to power two small cities.

AT HOME

The USS *John C. Stennis* sails into its home port of San Diego during Operation Enduring Freedom in 2002.

PROTECTION RACKET

The air shudders as an F14 Tomcat with full **afterburner** thunders off the deck. F14s provide hard-hitting combat fighter protection to the *Stennis* and other ships in the carrier group.

>> **afterburner** = a power boost using reheated exhaust gases

AIR WING

Crewmembers line the deck of the USS *John C. Stennis*. The aircraft are F/A 18 Hornets belonging to the 9th Air Wing.

ROCKET RIDE

"It's like driving a rocket ... it's the best amusement park ride you'll ever get on."

Andy Borwick, F/A18 pilot, USS *John C. Stennis*.

SUPER STING

The main strike weapon on board *Stennis* is the F/A18E/F Super Hornet. This updated version of the F/A18 has an automatic takeoff system. The pilot holds on to a handgrip on the **canopy,** while the airplane rises about 150 feet clear of the deck. Then the pilot takes over manual control.

>> **canopy** = a transparent cockpit cover

Carrier Enemies

ENEMIES UP ABOVE

British carrier-based S2 strike aircraft prepare to attack an "enemy" task force during NATO exercises in the Atlantic in the 1970s. If enemy aircraft penetrate the carrier's outer defense ring, they can cause great damage with missiles, air-launched torpedoes, or bombs.

An aircraft carrier is a **prime asset**, which also makes it a prize target. Aircraft carriers are extremely large and difficult to move around, especially if they are with a fleet of support ships. They cannot easily be made **stealthy.** The carrier is at risk from attack by aircraft, surface vessels, and submarines. It may have many defenses, but it also has many enemies.

ENEMIES ALL AROUND

A Matra Otomat surface-to-surface anti-ship missile. Enemy surface vessels cannot easily get close to a well-defended aircraft carrier. However, warships may still be able to fire missiles and torpedoes that work at long range.

>> **prime asset** = military term for vital equipment

Enemies Down Below

The greatest threat of all may lie beneath the ocean waves. Hunter-killer submarines are designed to attack without being detected. They are armed with torpedoes and missiles launched underwater. They are probably the carrier's most hard-to-find and hard hitting enemy.

BELOW THE LINE

A Mark 48 torpedo is loaded aboard a U.S. Navy nuclear-powered attack submarine. Torpedoes are especially dangerous to surface ships because they approach underwater. This makes them difficult to find.

Kamikaze

During World War II, Japanese navy pilots carried out suicide attacks against U.S. carriers in the Pacific. This was a desperate bid to halt U.S. progress toward Japan. Called "**kamikaze**," these pilots flew airplanes packed with explosives into U.S. warships. Carriers were the main targets.

DECK DIVE

Already ablaze from anti-aircraft fire, a Japanese kamikaze plows toward the deck of a U.S. aircraft carrier in the Pacific. Many kamikaze were shot down or missed their targets. But enough succeeded to cause serious damage to the Pacific Fleet.

A KAMIKAZE VIEW

"The sleek new heavy bomber had been transformed into something grotesque ... all the glass had been removed from the nose and tail and replaced with plywood. Most equipment, including bombsights, radio, co-pilot's seat, had been removed. There was no defensive armament. 'So I'm going to fly into battle on this....' An empty feeling spread within my heart."

Seiji Moriyama, kamikaze pilot, 1945

BOWING OUT

Kamikaze pilots pay homage to their emperor before flying to their deaths.

The Cost

From October 1944 to January 1945, kamikaze airplanes struck a total of 25 aircraft carriers, although only two were actually sunk. Many hundreds of U.S. personnel lost their lives. Morale among carrier crews was badly shaken up. But kamikaze attacks failed to prevent U.S. forces from closing in on Japan. The war ended after **atomic bombs** dropped on Hiroshima and Nagasaki persuaded Japan to surrender.

USS *BUNKER HILL*

Deck crew struggle to put out blazing fires on the carrier USS *Bunker Hill* after two Japanese suicide attacks in May 1945.

>> **atomic bomb** = a nuclear weapon causing massive destruction

Aircraft Carriers

Aircraft carriers symbolize a nation's military strength. They come in different shapes and sizes, depending on the type of aircraft they carry and the job they have to do. Aircraft carriers range from mighty nuclear-powered floating airbases to small helicopter-carrying assault ships. They all share the role of extending a country's fighting ability far beyond home territory.

USS *ENTERPRISE*

The nuclear-powered USS *Enterprise* enters Pearl Harbor. Completed in 1960, the *Enterprise* was the world's first nuclear-powered aircraft carrier and the largest ever to sail the seas. It is also the tallest (at 250 feet), longest, and fastest (more than 30 **knots**) carrier in the U.S. fleet.

Details:
Crew: Ship's Company: 1,350; Air Wing: 2,480
Length: 1,101 ft. 2 in.
Beam: 133 ft.
Propulsion: 8 x nuclear reactors, **4 shafts**
Max Speed: 33 kts.
Displacement: 89,600 tons
Aircraft: 85

USS WASP

The USS *Wasp* and other ships of its class are the largest amphibious ships in the world. Named in honor of previous ships that go back to the American Revolution, *Wasp* was commissioned in 1989. Besides aircraft, this class of carriers also carries up to six assault landing craft, depending on size.

Details:
Crew: Ship's Company: 1,108; Marines: 1,894
Length: 844 ft.
Beam: 106 ft.
Propulsion: 2 x 70,000 hp steam turbines, 2 shafts
Max Speed: 20 kts.
Displacement: 40,500 tons
Aircraft: variable, including Harrier jump jets and helicopters

USS JOHN F. KENNEDY

Named for the thirty-fifth president of the United States, the USS *John F. Kennedy* is an all-purpose multimission aircraft carrier commissioned in 1968. *Kennedy* has seen action against Libya in 1989, took part in Operation Desert Storm in 1991, and has since been active in the Arabian Sea.

Details:
Crew: Ship's Company: 3,117; Air Wing: 2,480
Length: 1,052 ft.
Beam: 130 ft.
Propulsion: 8 x boilers, 280,000 hp, 4 shafts
Max Speed: 30 kts.
Displacement: 82,000 tons
Aircraft: 85

Aircraft Carriers

USS *KITTY HAWK*

The USS *Kitty Hawk* was commissioned in 1961 but has seen extensive refits in 1977, 1981, 1987, and 1998. Named for the site of the Wright Brothers' first manned flight in 1903, *Kitty Hawk* was the first of three carriers in its class.

Details:
Crew: Ship's Company: 3,150; Air Wing: 2,480
Length: 1,062 ft. 6 in.
Beam: 130 ft.
Propulsion: 4 x 280,000 hp steam turbines, 4 shafts
Max Speed: 30 kts.
Displacement: 86,000 tons
Aircraft: 85

Carriers cost billions of dollars to build and can take several years to complete. As a result, they are designed to have long service lives. Most are expected to last 30 years. Major refits can add another 10 or 20 years to that figure.

USS *HARRY S. TRUMAN*

The carrier USS *Harry S. Truman*, named for the thirty-third president of the United States, was commissioned in 1998. It is the eighth Nimitz Class carrier, based at Norfolk, Virginia, and the last carrier commissioned in the twentieth century. A total of 10 Nimitz class carriers is proposed.

Details:
Crew: Ship's Company: 3,200; Air Wing: 2,480
Length: 1,092 ft. 2 in.
Beam: 134 ft.
Propulsion: 2 x nuclear reactors, 4 shafts
Max Speed: 30 kts.
Displacement: 97,000 tons
Aircraft: 85

CHARLES DE GAULLE

The *Charles de Gaulle* is one of the few full-sized modern aircraft carriers built outside the United States. Named after the former president of France and hero of World War II, *Charles de Gaulle* is the French navy's leading nuclear-powered warship.

Details:
Crew: 1,950, including Air Wing
Length: 858 ft.
Beam: 211 ft.
Propulsion: 2 x nuclear reactors, steam turbines, 2 shafts
Max Speed: 27 kts.
Displacement: 41,000 tons
Aircraft: 35–40

>> **displacement** = method of calculating a ship's weight

Future Carriers

The next generation of aircraft carriers will be equipped with new and different airplanes. They will also have simpler takeoff and landing systems, more defensive technology, and greater stealth. Aircraft that can take off or land vertically will become more widespread.

EVOLVED NIMITZ

The ninth Nimitz class carrier USS *Ronald Reagan* at its commissioning ceremony at Newport News, Virginia. The ninth and tenth carriers will include a range of state-of-the-art technologies that take them beyond the older models. These ships are called "Evolved Nimitz." They will have more efficient flight decks to improve safety and to increase the number of **sorties** flown.

>> **sortie** = a combat flight mission

Looking Ahead

Carrier Vessel Nuclear (CVN) X is a new class of nuclear-powered aircraft carriers that will remain in service for at least 50 years. The first of these carriers will enter the U.S. Navy fleet in about 2013. It will be equipped with the latest version of the F/A18 Hornet and the Joint Strike Fighter (JSF).

UACV

A model of the navy's unmanned aerial combat vehicle (UACV) at a navy test center. A new **Integrated Warfare System** will use computer technology. The system will make sure that the ship's defensive and strike capability work together.

Future Aircraft Carriers

Many people argued against continuing to build large carrier fleets after the collapse of the Soviet Union, the long-standing enemy of the United States, in 1991. Recent world events, however, have shown the effectiveness of having a carrier force able to meet the military and political challenges of the 2000s.

AFFORDABLE AIRPOWER

VSTOL carriers have the advantage of being smaller and less expensive to build than full-deck carriers. Using helicopters or variable-thrust airplanes, they do not require bulky catapult and arrester mechanisms. Most of Europe's navies are building this type of carrier for their future commitment to worldwide operations.

>> **jump jet** = slang for VTOL airplane

The new JSF will gradually replace the U.S. Navy's F/A18 Hornet strike aircraft and the U.S. Marine Corps' AV8 Harrier **jump jets**. JSF combines the hitting power of the Hornet with the versatility of the Harrier. The carrier version will make a short takeoff and will land vertically. It will perform much like the **F22 Raptor**, and will share some parts.

WHERE'S THE CARRIER?

"When word of crisis breaks out in Washington, it's no accident the first question that comes to everyone's lips is: where is the nearest carrier?"

Former president Bill Clinton, visiting the USS *Theodore Roosevelt*, 2001

Hardware at a Glance

ASW = anti-submarine warfare

CVN = carrier vessel nuclear

EW = electronic warfare

HARM = heat-seeking anti-radiation missile

HMS = Her/His Majesty's Ship

JSF = joint strike fighter

NATO = North Atlantic Treaty Organization

SEAL = Sea/Air/Land Special Forces

SLAM = submarine-launched anti-aircraft missile

U-boat = German submarine

UCAV = unmanned combat aerial vehicle

UN = United Nations

USS = United States Ship

VSTOL = vertical or short takeoff and landing

VTOL = vertical takeoff and landing

Further Reading & Websites

Bartlett, Richard. *United States Navy.* New York: Heinemann Library, 2003.

Chant, Christopher. *The History of the World's Warships.* New York: Book Sales, 2000.

Clancy, Tom. *Carrier: A Guided Tour of an Aircraft Carrier.* New York: Penguin USA, 2000.

Davis, Jacquelyn K. *CVX: A Smart Carrier for the New Era.* New York: Brassey's Inc, 1998.

Gaines, Ann Graham. *The Navy in Action.* Berkeley Heights, NJ: Enslow Publishing, 2001.

Grant, George. *Warships: from the Galley to the Present Day.* New York: Gramercy, 2001.

Holmes, Tony. *Combat Carriers: Flying Action on Carriers at Sea.* Osceola, WI: Motorbooks International, 1998.

Jordan, David. *Aircraft Carriers.* New York: Book Sales, 2002.

McGowan, Tom. *Carrier War: Aircraft Carriers in World War II.* Breckenridge, CO: Twenty-first Century Books, 2001.

Miller, D. M. O. *The Illustrated Directory of Warships.* Osceola, WI: Motorbooks International, 2001.

Roza, Greg. *The Incredible Story of Aircraft Carriers.* New York: PowerKids Press, 2004.

Wragg, David W. *Carrier Combat.* Annapolis, MD: U.S. Naval Institute, 1998.

Center of Military History <http://www.army.mil/cmh-pg>

Maritime National Park Association <http://www.maritime.org>

U.S. Marine Corps <http://www.usmc.mil>

Virtual Maritime Museums <http://www.maritimemuseums.net>

Places to Visit

You can see examples of some of the preserved aircraft carriers and carrier aircraft contained in this book by visiting the naval and maritime museums listed here.

Baltimore Maritime Museum, Baltimore, Maryland <www.baltomaritimemuseum.org>
Battleship Cove, Fall River, Massachusetts <www.battleshipcove.org>
Boston National Historical Park, Boston, Massachusetts <www.nps.gov/bost/>
Canadian War Museum. Ottawa, Ontario, Canada <www.civilization.ca/cwm/cwme.asp>
Great Lakes Naval Memorial & Museum, Muskegon, Michigan <www.silversides.org>
Hampton Roads Naval Museum, Norfolk, Virginia <www.hrnm.navy.mil/>
Independence Seaport Museum, Philadelphia, Pennsylvania <http://seaport.philly.com>
Intrepid Sea-Air-Space Museum, New York, New York <www.intrepidmuseum.org>
Louisiana Naval War Memorial, Baton Rouge, Louisiana <www.usskidd.com>
Maritime Command Museum, Halifax, Nova Scotia, Canada
    <www.pspmembers.com/marcommuseum/>
National Museum of Naval Aviation, Pensacola, Florida <www.naval-air.org>
New Jersey Naval Museum, Hackensack, New Jersey <www.njnm.com>
Patriots Point Naval & Maritime Museum, Mount Pleasant, South Carolina
    <www.state.sc.us/patpt/>
San Diego Aircraft Carrier Museum, San Diego, California <www.midway.org>
U.S. Naval Academy Museum, Annapolis, Maryland <www.usna.edu/museum>
USS *Forrestal* Museum, West River, Maryland <www.forrestal.org>
USS *Hornet* Museum, Alameda, California <www.uss-hornet.org>
USS *Lexington* Museum, Corpus Christi, Texas <www.usslexington.com>
USS *Saratoga* Museum Foundation, Providence, Rhode Island <www.saratogamuseum.org>
Vallejo Naval and Historical Museum, Vallejo, California <www.vallejomuseum.org>
Virginia War Museum, Newport News, Virginia <www.warmuseum.org>
Washington Navy Yard Museum, Washington, D.C.
    <www.history.navy.mil/branches/nhcorg8.htm>

Index

Picture Sources

BAe; 27, 44
Corel; 9, 10 (b), 14, 23
Defense Visual Information Center; 10 (t), 11 (t), 12, 15, 17, 19, 21, 22, 23 (c, b), 25, 28, 32, 35 (b), 36 (t), 37, 39
John Batchelor; 30–31
M K Dartford; 6, 7 (t), 26, 34 (b), 35 (t)
Robert Hunt Library; 7 (b), 13, 34 (t)

U.S. Navy; 4, 5, 8, 11 (b), 29, 31, 33, 41, 42, 43, 45